MY
WAY
OR
GOD'S
WILL?

The Choice is Yours

Brandi J-E McAlister, MS

Pat,
I pray this book is a tool you can reference
on your spiritual journey. When you choose
God's will over your ways that's the beginning
of doing life w/ God. It's a ride that's filled
with excitement, twists, turns, ups and downs
but it's all worth it ♡

7/3/2020

ISBN 978-1-7328197-8-8

This title is available as a BFF Publishing House Ebook.

Request for information should be addressed to:

praytheimpossible@gmail.com

Scripture quotations are taken from the Holy Bible, New International Version, NIV, Copyright 1973, 1978, 2011 by Biblica, Inc. All rights Reserved worldwide. The "NIV" and "New International Version" are trademarks registered in the United States Patent and Trademark Office by Biblica, Inc.

Scripture quotations marked NKJV New are from the New King James Version, Copyright 1982 by Thomas Nelson. All rights reserved.

Scripture quotations marked NLT are from the Holy Bible, New Living Translation. 1996, 2004, 2007, 2013, 2015 by Tyndale House Foundation. Tyndale House Publishers., Carol Stream, Illinois 60188. All rights reserved.

Any internet addresses, books, product or blogs are offered as a resource and not intended in any way to imply an endorsement by BFF Publishing House.

Cover Design: Thomas Teel

Photography: Mr. Brian Johnnson Productions

Printed in the United States of America

BFF Publishing House is a Limited Liability Corporation dedicated wholly to the appreciation and publication of children and adults for the advancement of diversification in literature.

For more information on publishing contact:

Antionette Mutcherson at
bff@bffpublishinghouse.com
Website: bffpublishinghouse.com
Published in the United States by
BFF Publishing House
Tallahassee, Florida First Edition, 2020

DEDICATION

This book is dedicated to everyone whose life I impacted through a single conversation by sharing my testimony, wisdom I gained through my own trials, and advice I provided from a godly perspective. I pray that this book will continue to be the encouragement you need based off of my real-life experiences. I pray that this book will be the starting point of letting go of self so that God can do work in you.

ACKNOWLEDGEMENT

God, I finally understand what You were doing. In 2018, I couldn't see what You were doing to me, through me, and for me. Over time, You gave me the clarity to see that Your plan was for me to let go of doing things my way so that I could do things Your way. In hindsight, the missing piece of the puzzle was understanding that what You wanted to accomplish in me was bigger than my plans for my life.

I needed to become who You called me to be. I needed to experience living life in its fullness according to Your promises. I needed to encounter things Your way, which is what's best for me. I needed to be in alignment with Your word to receive Your power and become a world changer. You needed me to be a voice in this generation to impact lives, one conversation at a time.

Thank you!!!

I love You,

BJEM

TABLE OF CONTENTS

INTRODUCTION

When I woke up on Sunday, September 15, 2019, I was able to discern that the atmosphere had shifted. I was excited to go to church, and this Sunday's service was like none other. Although my Pastor had previously prepared her Sunday word, the Holy Spirit showed up and took over. We praised and worshipped the entire service. I recall her saying, "You will not leave service the same way you came." You know what? She was right! The praise and worship I gave God was everything I needed, because I was tired the week before. I was tired of being spiritually attacked. I was tired of waiting on God to show up in a mighty way. I was tired of hearing "It'll happen when it's supposed to happen." I was tired of praying and believing and not seeing any manifestation behind my faith. I was tired of seeing other people receive their answered prayers and wondering when it was my turn. I was tired of doing well and not reaping the rewards that God promised. I was so tired that I reached a point where I took a moment to stand still and let God fight my battles.

After service, I was on fire. My spirit was lifted and I was excited to start my week. I was led to send NB his morning prayer that read, "Heavenly Father, thank You for hearing my heart's cry. I stand and intercede on behalf of NB. Transform his mind. Give him peace. Renew in him a clean and pure heart with a loyal spirit. Give him a heart that's filled with thanksgiving and gratitude. Help him to worship You with his entire being. Cast every spirit that's not of You out of him and off of him. Give him a spiritual awakening today. in Jesus' name, Amen. I was on a high from my worship and it felt so good to have a breakthrough. I just knew that nothing was going to bring me down from this mountaintop. Well, to my surprise, that high was going to be short-lived after the conversation with my dad. When I answered his phone call, I could tell by the tone of his voice where this conversation was headed. The conversation started with him venting to me about my brother. My spirit was not ready to deal with this negative energy, so I proceeded to change the topic by saying, "Okay, tell me something positive that you're doing." Since he was still grieving the loss of his brother, I knew he wouldn't be able to tell me anything positive. My spirit was now frustrated, saddened, and disappointed. I truly wished that he would apply the advice and encouragement I had given him.

After that conversation, I called my brother. By the tone of his voice, I could tell where the direction of *this* conversation was headed. Being the one that God chose in my family to influence and to keep everyone together, I had to put on my "little BIG sister" hat. My frustration led me to give some words of tough love. I said, "Listen. I don't know what you and your father have going on, but I'm gonna need for y'all to get it together. Enough is enough! I don't know what you're doing, but you need to man up and take accountability for your actions." My spirit just wanted to scream. I didn't even have the strength or the words to pray. I felt paralyzed. After a few minutes, all I could say was, "God, why can't they just get it together? I know it's in them. I want them to experience You in such a way that they have no choice but to do life the way You created them to, to do things Your way." For some reason, God had placed it on my heart to pray for them consistently this year. I had been praying for all three of them to draw closer to God; for God to transform them; for God to give them the desire to seek Him and become men of God.

Just when I thought I would take my Sunday nap to sleep off the heaviness on my spirit, God led me to help someone else. I posted an excerpt from conversation 15, "Purpose for the Pain," from my award-winning Devotional of the Year titled *Real Talk: A Conversation From My Heart To Yours.* One of my best friends commented and, unbeknownst to me, she would be the reason why I was led to post that excerpt. She said, "I'm just tired. I'm actually tired of being tired, if that makes sense?" I responded, "I know. Yes! It sure does. Have you still been praying?" She replied, "Just keep me in your prayers," to which I said, "Absolutely. You just gotta get back into a routine of just you and God. Speak to Him. In the shower. Your alone time. When you're headed to work or on lunch." She responded, "Yes, that's what's been missing. I have to start talking to Him again and start following His suggestions."

I tried to continue my nap, but my mind was racing. My spirit was unsettled because I wanted to help them. I remembered my minister telling me a few weeks prior that there are a lot of people who I have to help. Those words replayed in my mind over and over again. I tossed and turned until I got up and decided to go to Walmart for a notebook. Here I am, again penning a book from my heart to share my personal transformation—how I went from doing things my way to striving to do things according to God's will. I was unaware that the encounters I had with the four people mentioned, who are dear to my heart, were the reason that my atmosphere shifted that day. They needed my help, which is why my spirit was disrupted. Because of that disruption, I was moved to help you through my personal journey of letting go of doing things in my own strength and allowing God to have His way with me. My question is, are you going to do things your way or surrender to God's will? Remember, the choice is yours.

SURRENDER

How do you surrender to God's will when you've been doing things your way for years? Do you feel that God is calling you to surrender all? Are you scared to give up the life you know in order to surrender to God's will for your life?

The theme for my church in 2018 was G.L.O.W. (God's Light Operating Within): The Year of Manifestation, and I was so excited to see what God had in store for me. The theme made me want to do something different in my spiritual life, since I was a few months from my one year anniversary of being baptized. I decided on January 2, 2018, that I was going to write down goals that I sought to accomplish in my spiritual life. I wrote down the following:

1. Continue to grow and become a dope woman of God.

2. Continue to seek God and put Him first.

3. Higher level in God (speak out my praise and worship).

4. Continue to be a vessel for God to use me.

5. Tap into my power.

What I was not aware of was the power in my words. When writing these goals, I did not anticipate that a process would soon follow. I was in a great space in life and was on fire with writing what would become *Real Talk: A Conversation From My Heart To Yours*. I had six conversations written and remember saying out loud, "What else am I going to write about?" I remember clear as day hearing, "Don't worry. You'll have plenty to write about." I was getting ready to go on a ride of a lifetime and the month of January was the beginning of the end to my old self. That's when the shift suddenly happened. People close to me were starting to go through difficult situations and my difficult situation would soon follow.

I replayed in my mind a conversation with a friend I had three months prior, when I turned 33 years old. The conversation was about your "Jesus Year." She is a few years older than I am and she shared her experience with me. She said, "When you turn 33, it's life-changing. Jesus died at 33 years old, and his life was impacted in a major way, which is why it's often referred to as your Jesus Year. I had my daughter at 33 and that was life-changing for me." I was intrigued and expected God to do amazing things for me in my Jesus year, too. I thought about how one of my best friends got married two months after she turned 33, and how another best friend became a mother three months after she turned 33. I thought to myself, *Okay, maybe my life-changing experience will be getting married or starting my own family in my Jesus Year just like how God blessed them, since I'm also in a relationship. This is what I believe God will manifest in my life for 2018. That's life-changing right? What else would impact your life in a major way?*

What I thought would happen in my Jesus Year was not what God had planned for me, and that's when my difficult situation arose. Things swiftly started to go differently than I had planned and I became so confused, frustrated, angry, and disappointed with God. I was expecting my plans to come to fruition, but what I didn't understand then was that how I wanted things to manifest was not in the will of God, and that's when the pain set in. I did not understand at the time that God was allowing me to experience pain, confusion, and disappointment in order for me to surrender to Him. While I

15

was growing through the process filled with mixed emotions, I did not know at the time that was God's will for my life. He needed me to feel all the pain, just like my friends were experiencing pain in their lives, in order to finish writing the remaining conversations that would make the finished work authentic and relatable.

On April 18, 2018, I wrote in my journal "Woke up not in the best spirit. I prayed to God and surrendered all. I spoke to God about my hurts and disappointments about my experiences and what I thought was going to be. Last night I wrote about the next level in God (ready for the storm that comes before, but now that I look back, was I really ready? Be careful what you ask for; it just might come to pass). New wine can't go in old wine skin." I had a moment with God when I wrote, "I lay down my feelings, my personal hurts, causes and issues burning inside of me to align with your Kingdom." I had finally reached a point in my life where I realized that I needed to surrender my way for God's will. I acknowledged that asking God to use me as a vessel was bigger than my plans and my way of doing things.

I realized that my 2018 spiritual goals were the will of God for me. I was watching those words manifest at an unstoppable rate. Since I wrote down my goal to continue to seek God and put Him first, His will was overriding the plans I expected Him to do in the area of my relationship. I told Him, "I surrender. Not my will, but Your will be done." I know you're wondering, "How did you surrender?" I surrendered with tears in my eyes and my hands lifted up. I think that might have been one of the hardest things to do.

When you surrender to God, you are not aware of the things that you have to let go of, the process you will endure, or who you will become. You must truly let go of self and trust in God. In other words, it's a, "Jesus, take the wheel" kind of situation. Proverbs 16:9 NLT states, "We can make our plans, but the Lord determines our steps." I'm sure you've said to yourself "By now I should be married, have kids, have a house, work at this job, or making a certain salary." Have you ever considered that if it didn't happen when you planned for it to, that might not be God's will for you right now? Sometimes, we get in our own way and do not consider what God thinks about our plans. Perhaps the way you are going about trying to achieve your plans is out of alignment with God's will. No matter how hard you try to pray to God about it, if your ways do not align with God's will, He will not allow your plans to succeed.

IS IT MY WAY OR GOD'S WILL?

MY WAY IS:

Keep doing things you've already been doing, yet expecting different results.

Making plans on what you think is best for your life, then deciding to pray and ask God to bless your plan.

Walking in disobedience and expecting God to answer your prayers.

Getting upset when you don't see God blessing you with the desires of your heart that you've been praying about for years.

GOD'S WILL IS:

Matthew 6:33 NLT "Seek the kingdom of God above all else, and live righteously, and He will give you everything you need."

Jeremiah 38:18 NLT "But if you refuse to surrender, you will not escape."

Psalms 37:7 NLT "Be still in the presence of the Lord, and wait patiently for Him to act."

Leviticus 18:4 NLT "You must obey all my regulations and be careful to obey my decrees, for I am the Lord your God."

THE CHOICE IS YOURS:

Are you willing to surrender your ways for God's will?

CRY

God is waiting for you to cry out to Him. Sometimes we cry when we've done all we can do. Oftentimes, we cry first and then seek God as a last resort. God cares about all of us and He will use the choices we made that aren't in His will as a way to cry out to Him.

The moment I cried out to God to surrender my way for His will, I knew that this was the beginning of the end. During the beginning stages of my spiritual process when I let go of who I once knew, I found myself crying out to God more than ever. I couldn't comprehend that God was using my goals to orchestrate my spiritual transformation. I wasn't ready, nor was I prepared. While spending time with God, I began to reflect on the choices I made and the plans I held onto, as well as the things I did that weren't pleasing to God that caused some of my own heartache over the course of my life. In that moment, God imparted wisdom upon me and I was able to recognize that this was the content that He was referring to when He told me, "Don't worry. You'll have plenty to write about," earlier in the year.

Since I made the decision to surrender my life for God to use me, He had to give me a new foundation in Him that was teachable. The more I sought after God, the more He revealed through His word that I had never truly put Him first. He had to teach me how to truly seek Him and put Him first. He had to teach me that by spending time in His word, I will know and understand the will He has for me. God showed me that my way of wanting things was not aligned with His word. Although God showed me that I was learning from my mistakes, it was a constant reminder of how hard it was to let go of my old ways of thinking, believing, and living. I cried out to God because the process was challenging, painful, and uncomfortable.

My spirit was tired of doing things my way and plans not working out in my favor. Once I surrendered, I had no choice but to want to do things God's way. With my new foundation in God, I was starting to see that His way has power and my way was ineffective due to my lack of power. I had to align my life according to the word of God. Trust me—this is an ongoing process, and I have days where I still fall short. But what I *can* say is that it's easier today than it was a year ago. This was God's way to take me higher in Him so that I would eventually tap into the power I wrote down.

Nine times out of ten, our plans and the way we envision them do not align with God's will. Since God gives us free will, He gives us the choice to choose His way or our way. When we choose our way, which takes us off course, God sometimes will orchestrate or allow the enemy's plan to go forth, causing us to cry out to God for help. God is a good God and He wants to bless us with good and perfect gifts, but He will do it in His timing and in His way. I can attest that doing things God's way is hard!!!!! It's hard because it comes with spiritual attacks, warfare, isolation, the narrow road, and less of you and more of God.

IS IT MY WAY OR GOD'S WILL?

MY WAY IS:

Getting hurt because you expected things to go according to your plans.

Expecting God to answer prayers, but you never asked if this is what God has in store for you.

Crying because you are not seeing your answered prayers.

God allowing your decisions to become a disaster so that you can cry out to Him.

GOD'S WILL IS:

Psalms 57:2 NLT "I cry out to God the Most High, to God who will fulfill His purpose for me."

1 Chronicles 5:20 NLT "They cried out to God during the battle, and He answered their prayer because they trusted in Him."

Job 12:9 NLT "For they all know that my disaster has come from the hand of the Lord."

Deuteronomy 30:15 NLT "Now listen! Today, I am giving you a choice between life and death, between prosperity and disaster."

THE CHOICE IS YOURS:

Are you willing to cry out to God so that He can be in the driver's seat of your life?

SACRIFICE

What are some things that you are willing to sacrifice in order to receive the blessings God has for you? What are you willing to sacrifice to become the best version of yourself? I learned over time that God will require you to let go of the thing you want the most as a sacrifice to Him. It's not a sacrifice if it doesn't hurt. Making a sacrifice was never intended to be easy.

Ironically, on the one year anniversary of my baptism, I remember being in church. My Minister looked at me during service and said in front of the congregation, "God is changing your relationships and outcome because He is in need of you. Write down everything you want in a mate. Release your expectations. It's not going to look like what you think. Let God be God." I reflected on those words for weeks in a state of confusion and thought, *Well, hmm. Things have started to change in my relationship, but what is God in need of me to do? This doesn't even make sense.* With my lack of understanding at the time, I wasn't able to put the pieces together and realize that this was the manifestation of my wish for God to use me as a vessel. God needed me to not only finish writing *Real Talk,* but soon, I was going to take the next steps and publish it. So, what would God do in order for Him to accomplish that through me? What did God need me to do that would make me focus on Him and the assignment I subconsciously signed up for? What was the one thing that I wanted more than anything, that was standing in the way of me allowing God total access to use me a vessel?

As I spent more time with God and re-read what I wanted in a mate, it dawned on me that something was missing. I looked at my vision board I created in 2016 and realized God was nowhere to be found. I thought I had God in my relationship, but after experiencing God in a new way, I realized that He was not a part of it in the way He should have been. Just like my Minister mentioned about a month prior, things were changing in the relationship. Was God causing situations to happen within the relationship that were intended for me to let go of so that I could let God be God? Was God destroying the foundation I built based off of my ways before I knew how to do things according to God's will? Did God intentionally want the relationship to end because He was not being put first? Just when I thought things couldn't have gotten any worse I had to make a decision that I never thought that I would have considered.

Was God asking me to sacrifice the relationship that I prayed for so that He could fully use me as a vessel? Similar to the story in the Bible of Abraham sacrificing His son that he waited years for, was I, too, going to sacrifice my relationship that I've been waiting years for in order to go deeper in my relationship with God? Did God want me to sacrifice what I had already decided would be my life-changing event in my Jesus Year because I did not include Him in my plans, or was I going to strive to make things work in my own strength? Was I going to disregard that I asked to be a vessel because actually being a vessel didn't look the way I expected it to? Was I going to keep praying and asking God to bless what I built, that didn't include Him according to what His word says? I made the tough decision to sacrifice what I wanted most in life for God's will, not knowing what His plans were after that. I can tell you that it was a sacrifice because it hurt;it was something that I didn't want to do, but had to.

The only way to strengthen and have an authentic relationship with God was to be in a relationship with God and God alone. I thought I had a relationship with God, but I later learned that it was a surface-level relationship. As time went on, I slowly accepted that I needed a real relationship with God in order to fully walk into my calling and purpose. The new relationship I was building with God in my time of isolation and separation period was according to His will. I later realized that I couldn't afford to be distracted on this journey. I had to learn to let go and sacrifice things that were associated with my old ways of thinking and who I once was. I endured a process of unlearning everything I thought a relationship was according to society, and re-learned about a relationship that is pleasing to God. God needed me to impact lives one conversation at a time through *Real Talk,* and it was only possible through sacrifice.

I understood months down the road that the sacrifice was needed on so many levels. Over time, I learned that I was putting my heart's desires before God. God had to teach me through difficulties that I had no choice but to put Him first, above anything or anyone. God needed me to stop idolizing my heart's desires and focus on what He called me to do. God knew the sacrifice was going to hurt, and that was His strategy to get me to deepen my faith according to what I wrote down as a spiritual goal. Although I asked to be used as a vessel, I had to deal with every aspect that came along with the process. I came to terms with the importance of sacrificing things for God so that He can use me to do great things. Even though I had to sacrifice what I wanted more than anything, the spiritual rewards that God blessed me with can't even compare to the temporary pain I felt during the process.

Ultimately, God needed me to sacrifice my heart's desires so that He could give them to me in the way He wants me to desire them. My thoughts and desires were transformed; now, I to wanted them according to God's will for my life. Now, I can say without a shadow of a doubt that after praying for my desires according to God's will, my desires will come to fruition because He instilled them within me. He gave me my heart's desires in a way that has purpose attached to them. I now want God to get the glory from my desires because I know that my testimony will bless the lives of many. Isn't that God's will for our lives to be a blessing to others through the blessings He gives us?

IS IT MY WAY OR GOD'S WILL ?

MY WAY IS:

Holding onto something that is out of season.

Trying to make your heart's desires manifest, although it is the very thing God wants you to let go of.

Struggling with making a sacrifice in fear of God not blessing you in better ways.

Being scared to make a sacrifice because you do not know what God is going to do next.

GOD'S WILL IS:

Psalms 5:12 NET "Certainly You reward the godly, Like a shield you protect them in Your good favor."

Psalms 4:5 NLT " Offer sacrifices in the right spirit, and trust in the Lord."

Psalms 50:5 NLT "Bring my faithful people to me — those who made a covenant with me by giving sacrifices."

John 10:17 NLT "The Father loves me because I sacrifice my life so I may take it back again."

THE CHOICE IS YOURS:

Are you willing to sacrifice the one thing you want most in life to form or have a deeper relationship with God?

BEAR

Does it feel like your life is slipping through your fingers? Did you know that God will not give you more than you can bear? When you let go, surrender, and give it to God, then you will be able to bear it because He is with you. He will give you the supernatural power to bear anything that comes your way.

It kept resonating in my spirit, the word from the beginning of that year when my pastor shared with us the theme for our church. She said, "In order for God's light to shine, we have to be broken." Little did I know that the five spiritual goals I wrote 2 1/2 months into my Jesus Year would come with a cost that I had to bear. Throughout my process, I was constantly reminded of my Jesus Year and how Jesus had to bear things none of us could even imagine. Understanding and knowing God more and more each day, I realized that I was, in fact, experiencing things that were life-changing. So, what did I have to bear? I was bearing my version of crucifixion and brokenness so that God's light could operate within me. I had to bear releasing my former way of life, which included how I thought about things, how I prayed, how I spent time with God, and how I sought after God. God was breaking me so that He could build me up, but first, I had to learn how to bear the hurt and pain of struggling with the sacrifice I had to make. I had to let go of what I thought would be my life-changing Jesus Year moment, and bear the reality of what God's will was for my life then.

Throughout the duration of my alone time with God, My bedroom became my prayer closet. I traded in watching my guilty pleasure TV shows for watching sermons on YouTube.

Reading God's word in the Bible or devotionals on my Bible app aided in me being able to bear the assignment God set before me. I often thought about how during Jesus' 33rd year of life, He spent His time spreading the word of God. In my Jesus Year, I was doing that through Real Talk and through Pray the Impossible.

I was bearing the weight of being God's vessel to help people while enduring my own pain, hurt, and healing at the same time. For me, it felt like everything I once knew was crumbling before my eyes. My prayers I used to pray, dying to self and allowing God to work in me, changing the way I think— it felt as if I could not bear the transformation. Surrendering my thoughts, ways, and habits was no easy task. I had to be intentional about seeking God and His will for my life.

About 10 months after my conversation with my friend, I decided to look up the definition of Jesus Year to have a better understanding. I stumbled across this definition on Urban Dictionary: "Jesus Year is said to be the 33rd year of your life, where you are reborn in some sense. Perhaps a mid-life crisis, perhaps an ego death, perhaps the year where you abandon your old ways and start anew. Or, perhaps, you were affixed to a cross and came out on the other side." Less than two months from completing my Jesus Year, I had a spiritual awakening. Have you ever heard the saying, "When things fall apart, they're actually falling into place"? I am a witness— that is how God operates. When things are falling apart in your life, it's so that He can clear the path and get rid of the things that serve you no purpose. As things are falling apart, He will give you His strength to bear it while He works behind the scenes placing things together according to His will. I realized, What else could God use? How else could God get me to bear the cross I needed to advance toward becoming the dope woman of God I now know that He was molding and shaping me to be?

IS IT MY WAY OR GOD'S WILL?

MY WAY IS:

Holding onto the life you know in fear of the unknown.

Thinking this is the end of the world because your life appears to be falling apart.

Wanting to give up because you cannot bear the pain, hurt, and disappointments in your own strength.

GOD'S WILL IS:

Matthew 11:30 NLT "For my yoke is easy to bear, and the burden I give you is light."

Phillippians 4:13 NLT "For I can do all things through Christ who strengthens me."

Isaiah 40:31 NLT "But those who trust in the Lord will find new strength. They will soar high on wings like eagles. They will run and not grow weary. They will walk and not faint."

1 Corinthians 10:13 NET "No trial has overtaken you that is not faced by others. And God is faithful. He will not let you be tried beyond what you are able to bear."

THE CHOICE IS YOURS:

Are you willing to bear the weight of your mistakes from doing things your way in order for God to work through you?

HAPPENING

In the natural realm, it may seem as if life is happening to you because of the hardships you may be facing. Have you ever looked around and wondered, "What's happening?" Things are happening behind the scenes in the spiritual realm that God has yet to reveal to us. No matter what may or may not appear to be happening in your life, keep your eyes ahead of you and fixed on God.

"God, what's happening?" were words that I spoke out of confusion. I knew that I had asked to be used, but did that mean I had to endure a process of being pruned, purged, renewed, transformed, separated, isolated, and stripped of who I used to be for what seemed like an eternity? While I was growing, I had a hard time articulating to friends what was happening. I was well aware that some people wouldn't understand who I was becoming due to the way they viewed the world. I accepted that my transformation would be hard for some people to understand, but it wasn't meant for everyone to understand. I was learning that the more time I spent with God, the more He was making me more like Him. God was changing my thought process and how I viewed life. He was downloading wisdom and giving me revelations that blew my mind.

During my growing season, the only person I knew who would truly understand me and relate to me was my co-worker, who is also my friend and my spiritual counsel. I recall spending mornings in his office talking about God, sharing my testimonies, and receiving encouragement and the push needed when life didn't always make sense. I remembered one conversation during which he said, "But, B, I told you this two years ago when God told me to tell you that you are not the same woman and you cannot go back to who you used to be. God was going to cause you to accelerate and it wouldn't take long. I told you, everyone can't go where you're going."

I rolled my eyes and then laughed because he was right. He always assured me when I doubted myself that I was on the right track. He provided the wisdom I needed when I did not understand what was happening. He continued to speak the vision over my life when I could no longer see the light at the end of the tunnel. He was a constant voice from God that helped me to piece together that all of this was happening because people needed me. He constantly reminded me that no matter what was happening to me, through me, and for me, I was always birthing something.

In hindsight, although I did not know what was happening, everything that happened was for a reason much larger than me. Everything that happened was meant to make me the dope woman of God I anticipated becoming. Everything that happened was meant to transform me. Everything that happened was meant to take me to higher heights. Everything that happened gave me wisdom. Everything that happened made me relatable to those I would soon help. Everything that happened prepared me for what God had in store for me. Everything that happened gave me content for more devotionals, books, words of wisdom, and gems from my heart. Everything that happened allowed me to see God in a new way. Everything that happened was in alignment with God's plan to make my spiritual goals manifest. Everything that happened was meant to push me to strive to do things according to God's will for my life.

IS IT MY WAY OR GOD'S WILL?

MY WAY IS:

Going to friends for advice first instead of going to God first.

Not seeking wise counsel to provide you with godly wisdom.

Getting upset, frustrated, and mad when you are unable to understand what is happening.

Not knowing how to fight back when the enemy attacks.

Not believing that what is happening to you is for your good.

GOD'S WILL IS:

Romans 8:18 NLT "Yet what we suffer now is nothing compared to the glory He will reveal later."

Romans 8:28 NLT "And we know that God causes everything to work together for the good of those who love God and are called according to His purpose for them."

James 1:2 NLT "Dear brothers and sisters, when troubles of any kind come your way, consider it an opportunity for great joy."

THE CHOICE IS YOURS:

Are you willing to endure the obstacles, trials, and tribulations although you do not know or understand what's happening?

DETACH

Have you ever been so attached to your heart desires that you weren't open to detaching yourself from them? Did you know that when you detach from the things that you want, you are making room for God to give you what you need? Allowing yourself to detach from things that are less than God's best for you opens your mind, heart, and spirit to receive what you never thought was possible.

During this transition process, I was still slightly attached to the desires of my heart according to how I knew to desire them. Just when things appeared to have been coming into fruition, God made me sacrifice them for the greater good. The struggle with detaching ensued when I saw my desires manifest in the lives of other people. I had been praying for them for years; and my desires were deeply rooted in my heart and I knew they weren't going to go away in the blink of an eye. It was a constant battle because there were outside voices reminding me of the things I had prayed for. I saw people receive blessings that would be considered "out of the will of God", *so how was I any different from them? Why were they able to receive the same blessings while my prayers were at a standstill?* It was a trigger to my internal confusion and my inability to understand what good was going to come out of this. I later learned that because I asked to be used, God would bless me according to His will for Him to receive glory from my life.

The hardest part about detaching was trying to articulate an answer to the questions I felt bombarded with from those closest to me. How could I explain something spiritual that did not make sense naturally? How could I justify the true reasoning for the sacrifice I made and explain that it was because God was in need of me? Should I give a generic answer that would be easy for them to comprehend? How could I share my new knowledge that I needed to detach from my desires in order to receive them? How would I explain that God did not want me to desire things like the rest of the world did; that I needed to desire them the way God wanted me to? Since I was still trying to process what God was revealing to me, I knew that my loved ones wouldn't be able to recognize that I had to detach in order for God to birth His will in me.

Through my detachment, God was strengthening my relationship with Him. He revealed to me that I should not have compared the timing and appearance of others' blessings with the timing and appearance of my own blessings. He needed to empty me of the way I wanted and viewed things so that He could give me the wisdom and knowledge I needed to be who He created me to be. Once I reached a place where I accepted that there was a high calling on my life with great purpose, I was able to recognize that God was using me as a vessel to impact people in a new and refreshing way. I acknowledged the reason I had to detach from my heart desires was so that He could complete the work He began in me. I detached so that God could use me as an example of doing things His way, not my way. My detachment showed others what God is able to do when you let go of doing life your way and choose His will for your life. Most importantly, God revealed that I wanted my desires more than I wanted Him. The only way I was going to learn to want more of God was to detach from my ways, wants, and the way I desired things.

IS IT MY WAY OR GOD'S WILL?

MY WAY IS:

Saying, "I want what I want."

Allowing the pressure from outside influences to hold you back from detaching from your desires.

Not being open to receive what God wants to give you.

Wanting your desires according to society and not according to God's will.

GOD'S WILL IS:

Psalms 37:4 NLT "Take delight in the Lord and He will give you your heart's desires."

James 4:8 NLT "Draw near to God and He will draw near to you. Cleanse your hands, you sinners, and make your hearts pure, you double-minded."

Job 22:22 NLT "Listen to His instructions, and store them in your heart."

THE CHOICE IS YOURS:

What are you willing to detach from so that God can give you the desires of your heart?

DISAPPOINTED

Were there expectations that you had for your life and later found yourself disappointed because they weren't met? Or, maybe, you've been praying for something for years and it hasn't manifested yet, and now you're disappointed with God? Or, perhaps, you expected things to happen for you by now, and the disappointment set in when it didn't happen according to your timeline? Disappointments are a part of life. Sometimes, disappointments are necessary in order for you to shift your perspective from yourself to God. God will also allow disappointments in order for you to put your expectations on Him instead of your plans, another person, or a thing.

I remember being extremely disappointed with God. I was praying and seeking God at the level I knew at that time, and could not understand why my prayers were not being answered. *After all, God says that we can ask for anything and it will be granted, right? If that's the case, then how come my prayers aren't being answered?* is what I often wondered. I had to learn the hard way! Even though God says we can ask for anything, the key to asking is knowing that if it's not according to His will, your prayers will fall on deaf ears. What I didn't know was that I would spend more time waiting for my answered prayers than I expected. It took a while to fully grasp and understand what it meant to ask according to God's will and not my way. I later learned that I caused many of my own disappointments and then tried to blame them on God out of anger due to my lack of understanding.

When I reflected on my spiritual state, it was revealed to me that I never sat in the presence of God to see if what I wanted was what *He* wanted to give to me. I now know that what I wanted back then wasn't going to give Him the glory. The prayer requests were to benefit me, and since I asked God to use me, He had to work on me to get rid of selfish desires. It was a spiritual awakening when I realized that my desires were not going to help or benefit other people. How was God answering my prayers in the way *I* saw fit going to impact the lives of *others?* How was God going to give me a testimony that would glorify Him? I wasn't wrong for wanting my desires, but now, I had to change the way I wanted them. I often laugh and think that if God had granted my prayer requests two years ago, I would live happily ever after and not think twice about who needed my help. I wasn't concerned with who needed God's wisdom, who needed encouragement, and who needed to see God through me.

But now, I see what God was doing, and I'm thankful I surrendered my desire for it to be according to God's will. I would not have impacted as many lives as I have. I would not have known what it feels like to be a true blessing to others at this level. I would not have known what pure joy feels like when someone tells me how my book or gems from my heart have helped them. I'm grateful that my disappointments allowed me to see from God's perspective that He wanted me to glorify Him. Now I know that God's will never disappoints.

IS IT MY WAY OR GOD'S WILL?

MY WAY IS:

Asking God for things that will only benefit you.

Making plans for your life and not considering whether or not God ordained this for you.

Blaming God for the disappointments that you caused based off your own plans.

Not accepting that God's way is contrary to your way.

GOD'S WILL IS:

Proverbs 16:9 NET "A person plans his course, but the Lord directs his steps."

Matthew 5:6 NLT "In the same way, let your good deeds shine out for all to see, so that everyone will praise your heavenly Father."

THE CHOICE IS YOURS:

Are you willing to allow your disappointments to change your perspective from viewing things as the world views things in order to view life from God's perspective?

OBEDIENT

Have you ever thought that maybe you aren't seeing your answered prayer because you are not willing to be obedient? What if the very thing you want is tied up in your willingness to be obedient to God? If whatever you are doing in your will is not working out, it could be because God is waiting for you to be obedient and do things His way.

During the process, God had to check me on quite a few occasions. After spending time with Him and reading His word, He revealed to me that I was not being obedient. There are things God requires of you before He will bless you. All these years, although I learned to ask God for forgiveness of my sins, I never confessed my sins to Him. I remember reading Mark 11:25 NLT "But when you are praying, first forgive anyone you are holding a grudge against, so that your Father in heaven will forgive your sins too." I sat back and reflected over family, friends, those who I was no longer friends with, and those who hurt me and did me wrong, I came to terms that I needed to forgive them. I said out loud to God, "I forgive _____ for doing _____ to me and hurting me". I realized that it was not about them; it was about me and God. I no longer wanted to be the reason why some of my blessings were blocked. Is it easy to forgive? Absolutely NOT! I recognized that my blessings were greater than holding onto something that happened days, months, or years ago.

It was through that same scripture that God revealed that I was not walking righteously because of my disobedience. I looked back over my life at the things I wrongfully did and asked God to forgive me. I often asked God to reveal things to me that I couldn't remember so that I could continue to be forgiven.

Every time I remembered something that wasn't pleasing to God, whether it be my attitude towards someone, a habit, or an action, I confessed these sins out loud and received God's forgiveness. Similar to a parent and child, when we are disobedient to our parents, they discipline us by withholding things from us. I no longer wanted God, my heavenly Father, to withhold good things from me. I learned that when God instructs us to be obedient and we chose not to, we opt to delay our blessings. It's a hard process, but there are great rewards that yield from your obedience.

IS IT MY WAY OR GOD'S WILL?

MY WAY IS:

Holding onto a grudge towards someone who hurt you.

Not showing mercy to anyone who hurt you because you believe they don't deserve to be forgiven.

Not acknowledging the things you did wrong and seeking God to forgive you.

Not realizing that you block your own blessings because of your disobedience.

Knowing right from wrong but still choosing to do what you want to do.

GOD'S WILL IS:

Colossians 3:13 NLT "Make allowance for each other's faults, and forgive anyone who offends you. Remember, the Lord forgave you, so you must forgive others."

1 Peter 1:14 NLT "So, you must live as God's obedient children. Don't slip back into your old ways of living to satisfy your own desires. You didn't know any better then."

Romans 16:19 NLT "But everyone knows that you are obedient to the Lord.

This makes me happy. I want you to be wise in doing right and to stay innocent of any wrong."

THE CHOICE IS YOURS:

Are you willing to be obedient and apply God's word over your life?

FOCUS

Are you focused on God or your wants? Even though it may look like things aren't working in your favor, what are you focused on? Are you focused on what God called you to do, or are you focused on the setback? Focus on God and He will add everything your heart desires.

So now that I had surrendered to God, made a huge sacrifice, and detached from my heart's desires to focus on God, now what? What's next? I spent the next few weeks finishing writing *Real Talk*, spending time at home praising and praying, and watching Sarah Jakes Roberts and Mike Todd YouTube sermons to feed my inner man. God continued to pour into me as I spent time seeking and worshipping Him. I was content with my season of isolation. I finally became intentional about God and after writing 34 devotionals, I realized this was the book that was prophesied over me five months prior. Something suddenly came over me and I began to research how to publish a book. After researching several companies and setting a conference call with a representative, I was ready to publish my book. Although I received the information I needed, I stumbled upon negative reviews which did not sit well with my spirit.

One Saturday morning, I remembered that my Sorority Sister had published children's books. As I was scrolling on Instagram, God led me to reach out to her to inquire about publishing my book. What did I have to lose? Sisters are supposed to help one another, right? Little did I know, the message I sent her was a divine connection—it was a part of God's plan for us.

I said, "Hey, boo! Quick question: I'm in the process of writing a devotional book and wanted to know what publishing company did you work with to self-publish your books?

She responded, "Hey, love! Congratulations on the book. I started my own publishing company for the last book. Also, if you wanna consider publishing through my company, I'd love to provide you with some info."

What started out as seeking information about publishing my book turned into something bigger than me. This inquiry was the missing piece that linked my obedience to God's purpose. It was later revealed that I had to focus on God because He was using me to be her first client for the company she began. God knew that my obedience to Him was the key to the doors He would later open for her to publish over 30 authors.

Once I signed the contract, it was now time to focus on the remaining four devotionals to create my devotional website and brand, Pray the Impossible! I was slowly starting to see the light at the end of the tunnel, which was the motivation I needed. I was officially excited about what I was subconsciously birthing. I spent the next three months working behind the scenes with my Soror/Publisher editing the book, applying her feedback to become more vulnerable in certain conversations, and building a brand that would soon become my new lifestyle. God just needed me to focus on Him so that He could set the stage for what I was about to accomplish, the lives I would impact, and the example I was going to become.

IS IT MY WAY OR GOD'S WILL?

MY WAY IS:

Allowing distractions to take your eyes off of God.

Not spending time with God so that He can mold, shape, and develop who you need to become.

Not focusing on what God called you to do.

GOD'S WILL IS:

Phillippians 3:13 NLT "No, dear brothers and sisters, I have not achieved it, but I focus on this one thing, Forgetting the past and looking forward to what lies ahead."

Proverbs 3:6 NLT "Seek His will in all you do, and He will show you which path to take."

THE CHOICE IS YOURS

Are you willing to focus on God and be intentional with what He is calling you to do?

ALTAR

What are some things that you need to leave at the altar? Perhaps you need to leave worry, doubt, fear, anger, hurt, anxiety, disappointment, your will, resentment, and anything hindering your growth at the altar. When you choose to leave those things at the altar, God will give you His peace, healing, a new heart, a new mind, His love, hope, faith, a fresh start, and so much more.

It was Good Friday and Lent was almost over. I couldn't believe the transformation that was taking place within those weeks of fasting. After spending time with God and journaling for 45 days, I read a devotional about giving something up and nailing it to the cross. It spoke about how Jesus had to give it all up for our sake. I wondered, *Today is my day to give it all up. What was I going to give up? What was I going to nail to the cross?* As I sat at my altar with my journal in hand, God revealed to me what I needed to give up and leave at my altar.

On March 30, 2018, I wrote down the things that I was giving up once and for all:

Not praying in God's will! I will no longer be afraid to pray in God's will;

Not asking for the peace to be okay if what I'm asking for is

not in His will for me;

Trying to force, rush, and think I heard God say something; Not being still to listen and wait for what God wants to say to me;

Fear/Discouragement/Anxiety/Worry/Guilt/Embarrassment;

Thinking about what others might say;

Not wanting what God wants for me;

Not fully surrendering to God's will;

I declare and decree these things in the name of Jesus!

Not praying with and in authority/not believing with authority;

Not praising You with audible praise and worship;

Not speaking and declaring life over myself;

Not tapping into my power;

Not asking for discernment in my life and relationships with others;

Saying, "God, when is it my turn?"

Leaving things at the altar is not an easy task. I can say that I left most of these at the altar; I have to constantly remind myself not to revert back to some things. It is an ongoing process, especially when you are under a spiritual attack. We will fall at times, but we have the choice to decide to leave it there for good, no matter the situation.

IS IT MY WAY OR GOD'S WILL?

MY WAY IS:

Praying in your will and not in the authority that God gave you.

Trying to rush God and His timing.

Not surrendering to God's will.

Thinking your way is best and not wanting what God wants for you.

Holding onto things that are not helping you grow instead of giving it to God.

GOD'S WILL IS:

Psalms 145:2 NLT "I will praise you every day; yes, I will praise you forever."

Isaiah 55:9 NLT "For just as the Heavens are higher than the earth, so my ways are higher than your ways and my thoughts higher than your thoughts."

Ecclesiastes 3:1 NLT "For everything there is a season, a time for every activity under Heaven."

THE CHOICE IS YOURS:

What are you willing to leave at the altar in exchange for what God wants to give you?

WORSHIP

Can you still worship God when He calls a loved one home? Can you worship God through the dark days, or are you only able to worship God when He answers your prayers? Is your worship at an all time high when He's showering you with blessings? We should worship God whether we are good or if bad things are occurring because God is the same today, yesterday, and tomorrow. Worship God because of who He is, not for what He does.

I recall reading a devotional about true worship during the 2018 Lent season. It hit me! I was not truly worshipping God the way He created me to. I thanked God for the blessings He bestowed upon me, but I never really thanked Him for who He is. I wrote in my notebook, "Do I know Him? Who is God?" For the first time ever, I intentionally wrote God's characteristics. I stated:

God is Holy

Just in all His ways

Faithful/Faithful in all His ways

Love

Peace/Joy/Courage

He upholds all who are failing

My rock

Trains my hands for war and fingers for battle

Gracious & Merciful

Deliverer

Provider

Protector

Strength

Wisdom/Knowledge/Understanding

Healer

Great

Almighty

Majestic

Sovereign

Redeemer

Restorer

Perfects that concerning thing!

He's all of these things and more. Through that list, God revealed that I truly did not know *who* He is. Since I did know Him, how could I give Him true worship? I still fall short to give Him true praise, but I'm a work in progress. I've learned to say "Thank you, Jesus," instead of always asking for something. I understand that is one way to please God. Telling God how wonderful and mighty He is makes His heart fond of you. The only way to truly worship God is to spend time getting to know Him, not only of Him.

IS IT MY WAY OR GOD'S WILL?

MY WAY IS:

Seeking God for what He can do for you.

Only praising God so that He can bless you.

Worshipping God when it's convenient.

GOD'S WILL IS:

John 4:24 NLT "For God is spirit, so those who worship Him must worship Him in spirit and truth."

Psalms 100:2 NLT "Worship the Lord with gladness. Come before Him, singing with joy."

Psalms 34:1 NLT "I will praise the Lord at all times. I will constantly speak His praises."

THE CHOICE IS YOURS:

Are you willing to worship God even when life is going contrary to what you're praying for?

SERVE

Have you ever served on a committee for an organization? Or, perhaps, you serve on a ministry for your church? Or, maybe, you've had a chance to volunteer and serve food to the homeless? When we serve others, we should look at it as an opportunity to please God. God sent Jesus to serve, not to be served. We were created to serve and help one another.

Reflecting on my goals I wrote in 2017 and 2018, I asked God to use me as a vessel—He did that and more. I did not know what being used by God would entail, but I was subconsciously giving God my yes. In the midst of writing Real Talk, I realized that my trials and tribulations would be how God decided to use me. I would serve those who would later go through a similar experience by coaching and helping them with the content of my life's journey. God was using my testimony as my "yes" to serve, to spark the interest in people to start a relationship with Him, to change their habits, to let God heal them, and to have their own come to Jesus moments.

Unbeknownst to me, another way I would serve would be on the platform, Pray the Impossible. God was grooming and preparing me with the two. Every week, I consistently wrote—and still write—weekly conversational testimonies on my devotional website to encourage, inspire, and help readers. On my social media pages, I provide daily words of encouragement, excerpts from my book, and gems from my heart to uplift my followers' spirits. God has given me wisdom to share an on-time word with people who need to hear God in the midst of their storms. God called me to serve by interacting with people on my platform where they would, in turn, share with me how the spoken words have blessed their lives.

Doing the work God called you to do is hard. There are times when I'm tired and have to remind myself to rest and recharge. When you serve, you must understand that it's not about you—it's about other people. Putting others before yourself is one of the most selfless acts of humanity that one can perform. Serving is where you will find great joy, true peace, unexpected blessings, spiritual rewards, a deeper understanding of purpose, and a fulfilled life. *Isn't that what life's all about? Aren't we called to serve?*

IS IT MY WAY OR GOD'S WILL?

MY WAY IS:

Making life all about you.

Being selfish.

Not willing to put other people before you.

Expecting others to always help you.

GOD'S WILL IS:

Romans 12:7 NLT "If your gift is serving others, serve them well."

Phillippians 2:3 NLT "Don't be selfish, don't try to impress others. Be humble, thinking of others as better than yourselves."

John 15:13 NLT "There is no greater love than to lay down one's life for one's friends."

THE CHOICE IS YOURS:

Are you willing to put your selfish needs aside to serve God?

CONFUSED

Does life confuse you at times? Confusion is a mix of our thoughts, the thoughts the enemy plants in our mind, fear, doubt, worry, and anything else you can think of. God did not intend for you to go through life confused because He is not the author of confusion. When you're feeling confused, take a moment to pause and be still in God's presence. Ask God to remove all confusion from your mind, heart, and spirit so that you can hear Him clearly. In the midst of being confused, God will answer you and clear your mind.

2018 had its moments of confusion for sure. While doing the work God called me to do, confusion was setting in because I was not seeing what I was praying for. I was sowing seeds into prophetic words I received, paying tithes, and giving offerings because I expected God to perform the miracles I wanted. *After all, God, I surrendered. Now I'm striving to do things your way, so I should receive my blessings now, right? What happened to the desires of my heart, God?* I etched in my mind a timeline for when I thought my desires would manifest. When they did not meet my timing, I was hit with the harsh reality of God's timing is not my timing. God was manifesting the blessings according to His timing and His plan for my life during that season. What caused confusion was my inability to apply God's word to my life, which says there is seed, time, and harvest. Galatians 6:9 NLT states, "So let's not get tired of doing what is good. At just the right time we will reap a harvest if we don't give up." I was growing weary because the timing was not making sense to me.

Confusion constantly seemed to consume my mind because I was seeing other people being able to speak things into existence instantaneously and it seemed like the only words that were manifesting for me were related to my book and the goals I had written down. I knew God was more than capable of bringing things to pass; after all, I was seeing my book manifest at an accelerated pace.

My friend's blessings caused me to believe that my blessings could happen for me within a short time frame, as well. But my impatience toward accepting that my seeds needed time to fully develop kept getting the best of me. My timing mixed with hearing testimonies that encouraged my faith, and witnessing other people's blessings in what seemed like a short period of time, caused the spirit of confusion to turn my faith into doubt. The confusion was clouding my mind, which often led to me doubting God's word and struggling with my faith.

How come I couldn't speak my blessings into existence like I once did? There were obstacles internally and externally which stopped the fruition of my spoken words, and I just couldn't wrap it around my mind. I only allowed confusion to get the best of me because I expected God to bless me at a specific time. I later realized that the calling on my life needed to fully manifest before God could fulfill the other promises.

IS IT MY WAY OR GOD'S WILL?

MY WAY IS:

Putting a time limit on when God should bless you.

Becoming disappointed when God doesn't answer your prayers when you think He should.

Comparing the time frame of someone else's blessings to when you should be receiving your blessings.

Doubting what God promised you because you do not see the manifestation.

GOD'S WILL IS:

1 Corinthians 14:33 NLT "For God is not the author of confusion, but of peace."

Psalms 37:7 NLT "Be still in the presence of the Lord, and wait patiently for Him."

Galatians 6:4 NLT "Pay careful attention to your own work, for then you will get the satisfaction of a job well done and you won't need to compare yourself to anyone else."

Psalms 94:19 NLT "When doubts filled my mind, your comfort gave me renewed hope and cheer."

THE CHOICE IS YOURS:

Are you willing to press in and seek more of God in the midst of confusion?

REMEMBER

Are you in a season where it seems like God is not answering your prayers? Did you take the time to remember when God came through before and answered your heart's desires? Oftentimes while we are waiting, we can't seem to remember all the other times God blessed us in past seasons. Take a trip down memory lane and remember your blessings. Remembering past blessings can be used to fuel your faith while you are waiting on your answered prayers.

"The Lord will give you the desires of your heart" are words that played through my mind. In the midst of questioning if what I desired is what God has placed in my heart, He reminded me of the heart desires I had from 2006 that came to pass. My senior year in college, I wanted to become a member of Delta Sigma Theta Sorority, Inc.; however, due to circumstances I had no control over, it was not what God had for me at that time. In 2006 I recall saying, "I'm going to be a Delta before 2013!" For the next six years, I prayed, desired, and saw the signs which assured me that my heart still yearned for Delta. On April 29, 2012, I became a member of the illustrious organization, Delta Sigma Theta Sorority, Inc. I remembered the tears of joy and thankfulness that overcame me when my desire manifested. Over the course of what seemed like six long years, God did not forget me. He made good on the desire that never left my heart.

God constantly reminded me of that blessing and desire throughout my process last year. This blessing helped to ease my confusion when I remembered that it took God six years to make it happen. So, what was the difference with timing and the new desires of my heart? I felt the same way as I did with that desire, so God must have given it to me. I'm repeating the same pattern of believing, praying, and seeing signs to encourage me, so why is it harder to believe that He won't do the same thing again? This time, I was more mature in my spiritual walk, and God was elevating my faith and trust in Him. I knew that God was using this reminder to teach me that no matter how long it takes, He will answer me. He has reminded me that I will have a greater appreciation of the blessings because I've been working hard for them. He was teaching me that the desire never left my heart because it's a part of a bigger plan that He has in store for me.

God's word says, according to Psalms 37:4, "Take delight in the Lord and He will give you the desires of your heart." I can't even begin to tell you how many times I quoted that scripture over the past 14 years. This time, I understood the scripture in a new way. When you spend time with God and delight in Him, He will place in your heart what He wants you to desire. Although years may go by and you may try to shake the desire off you or give up on it, the desire is still secretly hidden in your heart. When God places the desire in your heart, He will bring it to pass in His perfect timing. He will allow memories of past blessings to encompass your mind and remind you to hold on to the desires, because He's going to come through for you—just like He did the last time.

IS IT MY WAY OR GOD'S WILL?

MY WAY IS:

Forgetting about the blessings God gave you before.

Doubting God will bring your heart's desires to pass.

Giving up on your heart's desires because they do not seem aligned with the timeline you set for them to manifest.

Not pushing past what you see in order to hold on to the promise God placed in your heart.

GOD'S WILL IS:

Psalms 77:11 NLT "But then I recall all you have done, O Lord, I remember your wonderful deeds of long ago."

Psalms 21:2 NLT "For you have given Him his heart's desires, you have withheld nothing he requested."

Psalms 20:4 NLT "May He grant your heart's desire, may He bring all your plans to pass."

THE CHOICE IS YOURS:

Are you willing to look past your current situation and remember all the times God has blessed you before?

PROCESS

Life is a process. Sometimes, the process hurts. Sometimes, the process is long. Sometimes, the process is confusing. The process is always working for your good. The process is meant to prune you of your ways, purge you of your old thoughts, and strip you of your habits. The process refines you, transforms you, molds you, and shapes you into the person God called you to be. The blessing is in the process not the final outcome.

As I endured my process throughout 2018, I realized that my process had officially begun on March 25, 2017. On that day, I was baptized in the muddy waters of my home church's pool in Augusta, Georgia. The Holy Spirit brought to my memory that I was baptized in the name of the Father, the Son, and the Holy Spirit. When I was submerged in the water and came up as a new person, I left my old self and ways underwater. The process helped me to see that my baptism was the initial start of me embracing God's will for my life. I realized through my isolation that my old ways, thoughts, and habits no longer served who I was becoming. The process was extremely difficult. I often struggled with letting go of the person I knew in order to become a person who I had no idea about. I wrestled with thoughts about what people would think of me because people were used to seeing the "turn up" side of me. I eventually came to terms with putting my alter ego, "Bdiva," aside for a little bit in order to walk in the anointing of Pray the Impossible. Every foundation that was built according to my way had to be destroyed and rebuilt according to God's will.

Even though the process was hard, painful, and tiresome, I did see the reward. The process gave me an authentic relationship with God. The process introduced me to my true self. The process forced me to walk in my purpose. The process changed my perspective to see things in a godly way. The process changed my prayer life. The process made me want things God's way because my way was no longer working in my favor. The process gave me content and experiences to include within the books God ordained for me to write, for the encouragement to share with others, and to make me the person God called me to be. I had a spiritual awakening when I realized that everything I experienced throughout my 33 years of life was a part of the process.

IS IT MY WAY OR GOD'S WILL?

MY WAY IS:

Refusing to allow the process to run its course.

Struggling to let go of your old self.

Quitting the process and returning to the old life you are familiar with.

GOD'S WILL IS:

2 Corinthians 5:17 NLT "This means that anyone who belongs to Christ has become a new person. The old life is gone, a new life has begun."

Romans 12:2 NLT "Don't copy the behavior and customs of this world, but let God transform you into a new person by changing the way you think. Then you will learn to know God's will for you, which is good and pleasing and perfect."

THE CHOICE IS YOURS:

Are you willing to allow the process to transform, renew, mold, and shape you into who God intended you to be?

TRANSITION

Which season of transition are you in? Maybe you're in the "fall" transition, where dead things are falling off because it's time to sow and plant new seeds. Or, perhaps, you're in the "winter" transition, where your days are dark and cold and your situation is barren. Could you be transitioning into your "spring," where you are seeing answered prayers and your situation is starting to bloom? Or, perhaps, you have transitioned into your "summer," where you are reaping the harvest from the seeds you planted in your fall season. No matter which phase of your transition you are experiencing, remember that it all serves a purpose.

Finally! I transitioned into the season where my blessings were chasing me down. After an intense season of dark days, not being able to see the light, months of isolation, praying and not receiving answers, self-reflection, struggles, confusion, and drawing closer to God, I was finally reaping the harvest that God promised me. On September 6, 2018, *Real Talk: A Conversation From My Heart To Yours, A 30 Day Devotional* awaited me on my doorstep. As I brought the boxes into my house, I screamed with excitement. I played "Won't He Do It" by Koryn Hawthorne and the lyrics, "You gon' look back and be so amazed," described my emotions in that moment! I couldn't believe that after nine months, I had birthed my greatest creation yet!

After months of transitioning, growing, and experiencing labor pains, holding my finished product made the process worth it. The growing pains became a distant memory once I looked back on my transition and remembered how I surrendered my way to God's will for me.

Since I experienced many dark days, it was hard to discern what season I was in. I prayed for it to be my winning season when it was a season of growth. I was not aware that my fall and winter seasons were meant to transition me into my purpose of becoming an author and an entrepreneur. But now, the appointed time arrived for me to reap the harvest from the seeds I sowed. I couldn't believe that my harvest season was filled with opportunities I didn't have to pray for because God had them find me. I had two book signings, went on a book tour, was on a podcast, and was a featured guest on a radio show, just to name a few of my seeds. It was a breath of fresh air to see my hard work paid off.

IS IT MY WAY OR GOD'S WILL?

MY WAY IS:

Praying for things and expecting the harvest out of season.

Rushing to get out of the transition and enter the season of blessings.

Wondering when the season of dark days will be over instead of focusing on the area of growth.

GOD'S WILL IS:

Ecclesiates 3:1 NET "For everything there is an appointed time, and an appointed time for every activity on earth."

Leviticus 26:3-5 MSG "If you live by my decrees and obediently keep my commandments, I will send the rains in their seasons, the ground will yield its crops and the trees of the field their fruit. You will thresh until the grape harvest and the grape harvest will continue until planting time. You'll have more than enough to eat and will live safe and secure in your land."

Isaiah 43:19 NLT "For I am about to do something new. See, I have already begun! Do you not see it? I will make a pathway through the wilderness. I will create rivers in the dry land."

THE CHOICE IS YOURS:

Are you willing to allow the transition of each season serve its purpose by teaching you what you need to learn? Are you willing to apply these lessons to the next season of your life?

CONNECTED

Who are you connected to? Are you connected to people who talk about vision? Are you connected to people who push you to be better? Choose to be connected with like-minded people. Being connected to the right people will help you align your life path to greatness. When you surrender your ways in exchange for God's will, He is able to connect you with the right people.

God connected me with people who I thought would never become some of my greatest friends for His greater purpose. One connection in particular, which started out as a high school associate messaging me on Facebook to be a guest on his podcast when I launched the book, turned out to be another divine connection. His podcast was the first place where I discussed my book, shared my journey, and opened up about my struggles with being my alter ego "Bdiva and Pray the Impossible." After the show, I'll never forget the words he spoke over my life. He said, "B, I think you are the bridge between people who look like you and God." Those words touched my life in a way that confirmed my struggle. He was the first person to see what God was doing through me. He was able to see that God was doing a new thing to reach people in this generation. He was able to recognize that God was using me, the "turn up queen," to bridge the gap between Him and people who do not have a relationship with God, do not know God, or who are also struggling on their spiritual walks.

This was a connection I never saw coming and has been one of the greatest additions to my life. God divinely connected us; this high school associate became my photographer, suggests ideas to build my brand, and consistently pushes me out of my comfort zone to reach higher heights. Since there is a greater purpose for my life, God is using the gifts He gave my friend to influence me, enhance my skills, and help me to tap into the creative side that lies dormant inside of me. This connection is still helping me think outside of the box, work hard for my future, and grow as both a businesswoman and a brand. I believe that God connected us in order for him to help position me, prepare me for the big stage, and bring God's vision for me to life. God needed to use who I least expected to impact my life in ways I never imagined. Not only was this connection for me, it was a connection that he also needed. He was able to see God through me in a new way. God was using me to help him push himself to his highest potential and not doubt his own skills and capabilities. Our God-filled conversations help both of us dream bigger, see beyond our current situations, and to get to the top.

God revealed that *Real Talk*, Pray the Impossible, and Heart to Heart created connections with people that I knew in passing, as well as with total strangers. I connected with people who needed to experience God, see God's hand at work, and draw closer to Him. I often sat back in awe thinking, *What if I held onto my ways? I wouldn't even be this version of myself. I would have not experienced God in the way I did. I never would have connected with the right people to do God's work. God would not have been able to use me to bridge the gap and bring people closer to Him.*

IS IT MY WAY OR GOD'S WILL?

MY WILL IS:

Saying, "No new friends."

Not being open to who God wants to send your way to help you.

Being comfortable with your current circle.

GOD'S WILL IS:

Proverbs 27:17 NLT "As iron sharpens iron, so a friend sharpens a friend."

1 Thessalonians 4:18 NLT "So, encourage each other with these words."

1 Corinthians 12: 7 NLT "A spiritual gift is given to each of us so we can help each other."

THE CHOICE IS YOURS:

Are you willing to allow God to connect you with people who can not only help you, but also help bring God's greater plan into fruition?

PURPOSE

Do you know that we all have a purpose? Going through life you may tend to ask yourself, "What's my purpose?" but did you know that we all have gifts which lead us to our purpose? Think about what you are really good at. Whatever comes to mind could be your purpose.

During the process of writing my book and becoming who I was destined to be, Pray the Impossible was birthed. My original plan was to feature one of my written devotionals as a guest blogger on another devotional website, since I had so much content that I was not going to include in the book. One day, I shared my idea with one of my best friends, she said, "God is too much inside of you for anything small. You just wanted to write, but God wants you to do bigger things. You need to create your own devotional website and gain a following so that when your book comes out, people already know about you." Was this God using her to tell me His plans for me? After all, I did have four remaining devotionals from when I was writing the book.

At 7:13 a.m. on June 5, 2018, I hit the send button and launched Pray the Impossible. I was scared, nervous, anxious and worried about whether or not people would like it. Shortly after that, another friend suggested that I create social media pages to post words of the day to encourage people. I did not want people to know that it was me, BUT with God, it became the best part of me.

Pray the Impossible was who God was preparing me to be. With no intentions of it becoming a devotional website where I feature weekly conversational testimonies, this is the platform that introduced me to the world as a Spiritual Friendvisor (a friend who gives advice based off of godly wisdom). Just three months after my launch, while on my September book tour, I experienced a life-changing testimony. My sister in Christ approached my table where I was selling copies of my book. She had a binder in her hand, and on my table she laid printed copies of every devotional I wrote from June to September 2018.

I was shocked and in awe as she shared with me how she almost gave up. She had received my introductory email which launched Pray the Impossible and it saved her life. She told me about how she had been feeling really down and didn't know how she was going to make it. She told me that she had a God moment and was led to my website to start reading and downloading the devotionals. Her words, "You saved my life because I almost gave up," touched my soul and gave me a spiritual awakening.

"WOW. I saved her life. I know my purpose. I know what I'm doing in life. It's helping people," are words I shared on an Instagram video post. I discovered my purpose in life in 2016 when wrote in my journal, "I love encouraging people and sharing God's wisdom." Yes, I discovered my purpose, but I did not start living in my purpose until the second half of 2018. This was a part of God's perfect timing for my life. Every event I experienced was a building block, destined to give me experiences and wisdom to share with the world. In that moment, I knew that the calling on my life was much bigger than me doing things my way.

I thought to myself, *What if i didn't surrender my selfish desires for God's will for my life? What would have happened to her if I didn't create Pray the Impossible? Whose lives would have not been impacted because of my obedience to God's calling?* I knew my purpose was to impact lives, one conversation at a time.

IS IT MY WAY OR GOD'S WILL?

MY WAY IS:

Not surrendering to God's purpose, will, and plans for your life.

Not spending time with God to discover your purpose.

Not recognizing that your purpose is connected to the lives of others.

Deciding to be disobedient because of your own selfish desire.

GOD'S WILL IS:

1 Corinthians 12:7 NLT "A spiritual gift is given to each of us so we can help each other."

1 Samuel 15:22 NLT "What is more pleasing to the Lord; your burnt offerings and sacrifices or your obedience to His voice?"

Proverbs 19: 21 NLT "You can make many plans, but the Lord's purpose will prevail."

THE CHOICE IS YOURS:

Are you willing to let go of who you are in order to become who God is calling you to be and walk in your purpose?

I AM

I am loved. I am a child of God. I am blessed. I am highly favored. I am at peace. I am content. I am nothing without God. I am filled with joy. I am strong. I am wealthy. I am healthy. I am breaking generational curses. I am whole. I am complete. When you surrender to God's will, you become these things. When you allow God to complete a work in you, you can say "I am" because God is in you.

After a year of surviving the pruning, the purging, the process, the refining, the transformation, and the renewing of self, God revealed to me who I am in Him. I decided to write down affirmations for 2019 to remind myself who I am and whose I am. On January 5, 2019, I wrote:

"I am whole. I am healed. I am a child of God. I am anointed. I am chosen. I am blessed. I am highly favored. I am filled with joy. I am strong. I am filled with God's power and authority. I am a Spiritual Friendvisor. I am an influencer. I am encouraging. I am loved and loving. I am wealthy. I am confident in God's words. I am a voice that needs to be heard in this generation. I am a leader. I am physically, mentally, spiritually, and emotionally healthy. I am a praying woman. I am a wife of the word. I am a praying mother. I am a woman of God walking in divine favor. I am unique in what God called me to do. I am walking in radical faith."

It is important to call forth things that you desire as if you have already received them. You become what you say you are. I am all of these things because I affirm that I am.

IS IT MY WAY OR GOD'S WILL?

MY WAY IS:

Not speaking highly of yourself.

Allowing what other people say about you determine who you say you are.

Not knowing your true identity.

Allowing past hurtful experiences to shape and mold who you are.

GOD'S WILL IS:

1 Peter 2:10 NLT "Once you had no identity as a people, now you are God's people."

John 9:5 NLT "But while I am here in the world, I am the light of the world."

Psalms 116:16 NLT "O Lord, I am your servant. Yes, I am your servant, born into your household, you have freed me from my chains."

THE CHOICE IS YOURS:

Are you willing to call forth things that are not and declare you who are in God?

WAITING

God is waiting. He's waiting for you to put Him first. He's waiting for you to get out of your own way. He's waiting for you to stop idolizing relationships, careers, and materialistic things. He's waiting for you to put all your trust in Him. He's waiting for you to surrender your wants for what He wants for you. He's waiting for you to step out on faith. He's waiting to order your steps. He's waiting for you to forgive. He's waiting to use you. God is waiting for you.

Sometime in 2019, I heard the song "You Waited" by Travis Greene. As I listened to the lyrics, I cried out. I realized that all this time, God was waiting on me to surrender my way for His will. Doing things God's way was, and is, difficult at times because it's a constant battle between my flesh (my way) and the Spirit (God's will). There were plenty of days where I wanted to give up and do things my way, but then I would remember that God didn't bring me this far to leave me. All God ever wanted was to use me to do His will. He chose me and knew I would be able to get His work done, but He had to wait for me to come to my senses and come to Him with my all. God was so kind to wait until I got tired of doing things my way. He waited because He knew I would reach this point where I would see the bigger picture He has for my life.

Since God waited for me, I, in turn, had to wait for God to complete the work He began in me. I had to wait, go through the process, and undergo transformation to find and become the person God created me to be. I often found myself wanting to rush through the days, weeks, months, and seasons to get to the rewards. But God knew I was not ready, nor did I have the capacity to carry the weight of my anointing and purpose. God loved me so much that He waited for me through my mess, mistakes, shortcomings, disobedience, and sinful ways. His purpose for my life was predestined from when I was in my mother's womb. Whether He had to wait a day or years for me to realize that His way is what's best for me, His plan was going to come to pass.

IS IT MY WAY OR GOD'S WILL?

MY WAY IS:

God, I surrender all.

God, I want what You want for me.

God, Your will is what's best for me.

God, I don't know what You are doing, but I trust You.

GOD'S WILL IS:

Isaiah 40:31 NKJV "But those who wait on the Lord shall renew their strength."

Psalms 27:14 NLT "Wait patiently for the Lord. Be brave and courageous. Yes, wait patiently for the Lord."

Isaiah 30:18 NLT "So the Lord must wait for you to come to Him so He can show you His love and compassion. For the Lord is a faithful God. Blessed are those who ask for His help."

THE CHOICE IS YOURS:

Are you willing to wait on God to complete the work He wants to begin in you, no matter how long, hard, or confusing the transformation is?

REFLECTION

Self-reflection is imperative when monitoring your growth and transformation. During every season of our lives, we should reflect on who we once were, who we are, who we want to be, and where we want to go. Does your walk reflect your talk? Does your life reflect who God has called you to be? If you want to be all that you can be, then your mind, heart, body, and spirit should reflect your desired outcome.

After everything I experienced in 2018, I sat back and reflected on the word "courage." Earlier that year, I decided that would be the word I focused on for the year. At the time, I thought that courage meant praying bigger prayers, dreaming bigger dreams, and expecting bigger blessings. As I did a self-reflection over the past 11 months in my Jesus Year, I knew that courage represented another meaning. After I beared my cross of being broken in order for my light to shine, after what seemed like the longest season of opposition I had ever faced, I remembered that I had written down specific goals that I wanted to manifest during the year. I was neither ready nor prepared for what I had written into existence:

1. Continue to grow and be a dope woman of God.
2. Continue to seek God and put Him first.
3. Higher level in God by speaking out my praise and worship.
4. Continue to be a vessel for God to use me.
5. Tap into my Power.

I said to myself, *Remember, you wrote down these goals and God manifested them. You asked to continue to grow and become a dope woman of God. How else do you grow? You grow through the trials, tests, opposition, disappointments, and pain. When you come out on the other side, that's when you will be the dope woman of God you said you wanted to be.* Then, I told myself to continue to seek God and put Him first. I later realized that God had to isolate me. He had to set me apart from others so that the distractions could be removed from my life. God needed me by myself to complete the work that He began in me. God had to send oppositions my way that were contrary to what I was praying for. These oppositions left me no choice but to get into a God zone. I asked myself, *Oh, you forgot that you asked God to take you into a higher level in Him?* So, because I asked to go to a new level, I couldn't keep expecting God to bless me in the same ways that He did on the previous levels. God wanted to show me new blessings in a new way, and in a new dimension. In a deep state of self reflection, I told myself, *But, Brandi, you stated to continue to be a vessel for God to use you!* Well, this is the revelation that I wasn't really ready for.

God reminded me that I had asked to go to a higher level in Him, so He had to magnify the way He wanted to use me. I always had a passion for posting inspirational words on social media to help other people. He revealed how I was now going to do it through Pray the Impossible (my devotional website and social media page). He has given me the gift of encouraging people in my circle through my testimonial conversations, and now it was time to publish *Real Talk: A Conversation From My Heart to Yours* to reach and help people who were not in my circle. Last but not least, I said that I wanted to tap into my Power. March 25, 2017, I was baptized in the name of the Father, the Son, and the Holy Spirit, and NOW I feel the power that I was baptized in. In December of 2017, My Pastor asked me to give a word. I was obedient and gave the Sunday word, but was scared to look at the video right away. People told me that I did a really good job, but I wanted to wait until my one year anniversary of my baptism to watch it. On March 25, 2018, it blew my mind that I was witnessing what people have been telling me about myself for quite some time. I did not realize how encouraging the word was and the power that I possess to inspire people.

These goals came with a cost that I struggled with for months. Never had I experienced such a long period of time where my faith was being tested. I could not wrap my mind around what was happening to me. I didn't understand or grasp the person I was becoming. But I knew this was the assignment that God gave me and everyone would not understand. I didn't even understand it as I was growing through until recently. After I spent time reflecting, I remembered that I did ask God to do a new thing in my life. It was a cross that I later learned I had to carry. God had to "break" me in order for my light to shine. Were there other goals that I wrote down in other areas of my life? Absolutely! But when I specifically wrote down "put God first," He handled my goals in the order that was the way He saw fit for my life. The things dealing with doing His work and His will without a doubt had to come first. I now have a new understanding of the scripture Matthew 6:33, "But seek first the kingdom of God and His righteousness, and all these things shall be added to you." I now understand that when God places an assignment on your life, that must be completed first. He will add your rewards, the desires of your heart, and blessings afterwards.

So, after my conversation with God and my self-reflection, He showed me what courage really meant for me during that year. I literally saw a quote on social media right after that said, "You can't get to courage without walking through vulnerability." I thought, *WOW. I had to reveal my vulnerable side in writing my book, my devotional website and social media pages in order for God to use me as His vessel at this new level.* In order for God's will for my life to have been fully accomplished, I had to experience some Jesus Year moments that broke me from doing things my way to now living according to His will. Now, *that's* courage.

After 12 long months, I realized that I got married and started a family which has impacted my life in a major way. I married God's will for my life. I was married to spending quality time with Him. I was married to my calling. I was married to the new person I had transformed into. I birthed *Real Talk: A Conversation From My Heart to Yours*—after all, it did take nine months to write and publish the book. I gave birth to my purpose. I birthed my company and brand, Pray the Impossible. I birthed a platform where people who were looking for God, encouragement, hope, and faith would become family of Pray the Impossible. In the end, what I thought would be my Jesus Year life-changing moments came to fruition, but not in the way I imagined.

IS IT MY WAY OR GOD'S WILL?

MY WAY IS:

Reflecting on what God isn't bringing to pass in your life.

Thinking about what you desire and not learning from the lessons that come before the manifestations.

Not partnering with God during the transformation process to grow mentally, spiritually, and emotionally.

GOD'S WILL IS:

Proverbs 27:19 NLT "As a face is reflected in water, so the heart reflects the real person."

Psalms 119:5 NLT "Oh, that my actions would consistently *reflect* your decrees!"

Psalms 119:55 NLT "I *reflect* at night on who you are, O Lord; therefore, I obey your instructions."

THE CHOICE IS YOURS:

Are you willing to reflect over the years of your life to see that the hardships, process, setbacks, pruning, purging, and transformation served a purpose for you to do things God's way?

GOD'S WILL IS WHAT'S BEST FOR ME

God's will is for us to put Him first and keep Him first above any person, desire, and previous blessings you received. God's will is for us to have an authentic and genuine relationship with Him. God's will is for us to spend quality time with Him so that we know His character. God's will is for us to read His word so that we can be transformed. God's will is for us to apply His word to our lives so that our minds can be renewed, our hearts made pure, and our spirits made whole to be more like Him. God's will is for us to walk in obedience so that we do not have to experience the consequences from our choices that lead to disobedience. God's will is for us to praise and worship Him for who He is, not what He can do for us. God's will is for us to love Him with our whole heart. God's will is for us to rejoice in Him and in His goodness.

God's will is for us not to worry, because He wants us to cast all our cares and worries unto Him. God's will is for us to count all of our experiences as joy, no matter what life throws our way. God's will is for us to be delivered from our past. God's will is for us to be free from every stronghold that's on our life. God's will is for us to break every chain that's holding us bound. God's will is for us to know this battle is not ours, but the Lord's. God's will is for us to trust that He has already taken care of everything that concerns us. God's will is to walk by faith, not by sight. God's will is for us to think positive thoughts. God's will is for us to speak life over ourselves and our situations. God's will is for us to let go of doing life our way and to do life His way.

When you choose to do things God's way, you will experience a process. He has to empty you of you, transform your thoughts, renew your mind, create in you a clean and pure and heart, purge you, test you, and trust you. Deciding to live according to God's will comes with attacks, obstacles, trials, tribulations, and storms. These internal and external forces are necessary for Him to mold and shape you into His image. You will eventually begin to think like Him, speak like Him, and view life from His perspective; you will ultimately live and walk in your purpose and calling. Every season will be different and have its set of challenges because God is calling you higher and deeper in Him.

You will fall down, but God will wait for you to dust yourself off and get back up. He will continue to reveal His will for you at each new level with Him. Every level will demand a new version of yourself, so you have to remember to push past how you feel, what the transformation looks like, or what may come your way. The goal is for God's will to become your lifestyle, because doing things your way would be settling for less than the abundant life God wants you to have.

GOD'S WILL IS:

2 Corinthians 5:17 NLT "This means that anyone who belongs to Christ has become a new person. The old life is gone; a new life has begun!"

Romans 12:2 NLT "Don't copy the behavior and customs of this world, but let God transform you into a new person by changing the way you think. Then you will learn to know God's will for you, which is good and pleasing and perfect."

James 1:2-4 NLT "Dear brothers and sisters, when troubles of any kind come your way, consider it an opportunity for great joy. For you know that when your faith is tested, your endurance has a chance to grow. So let it grow, for when your endurance is fully developed, you will be perfect and complete, needing nothing."

2 Corinthians 5:7 NET "For we live *by faith*, not *by sight*."

2 Corinthians 10:4 NET "For the weapons of our warfare are not human weapons, but are made powerful by God for tearing down strongholds."

John 8:36 NET "So if the son sets you *free*, you will be really *free.*

Romans 15: 32 NLT "Then, by the will of God, I will be able to come to you with a joyful heart, and will be an encouragement to each other."

John 10:10 NKJV "I have come that you may have life, and that you may have it more abundantly."

Luke 22:42 NLT "Father, if You are willing, please take this cup of suffering away from me. Yet, I want Your will to be done, not mine."

"But, B, I told you this two years ago when God told me to tell you that you are not the same woman and you cannot go back to who you used to be" ~ M. Peek

"B, I think you are the bridge between people who look like you and God."~ B. Johnson

THE CHOICE IS YOURS:

Are you willing to live according to God's will?

ABOUT THE AUTHOR

Brandi J- E McAlister, MS is an award-winning author of the Devotional of the Year titled *Real Talk: A Conversation From My Heart To Yours,* self-proclaimed Spiritual Friendvisor of Pray the Impossible, and host of Heart to Heart on Instagram Live. Through her spiritual journey, she stands by her life motto, "Impacting lives one conversation at a time."

She learned through her transformation that God chose her for this unique assignment because she's relatable; she is what this generation needs in order to see and experience God in a new way. She prides herself in showing others that you can be authentic, walk in your purpose, live life to the fullest, turn up, and still love and serve God in the exclusive way He's called you.

You can experience more of Brandi's godly wisdom on www.praytheimpossible.com, where she shares weekly conversational testimonies, as well as on her Pray the Impossible Instagram Live show, "Heart to Heart," where she has real talk and she drops gems from her heart.

Made in the USA
Middletown, DE
28 June 2020

10224681R00060